Sue and Jule are pals.
Jule is Sue's grandma.
Sue and Jule like to mine for gems.

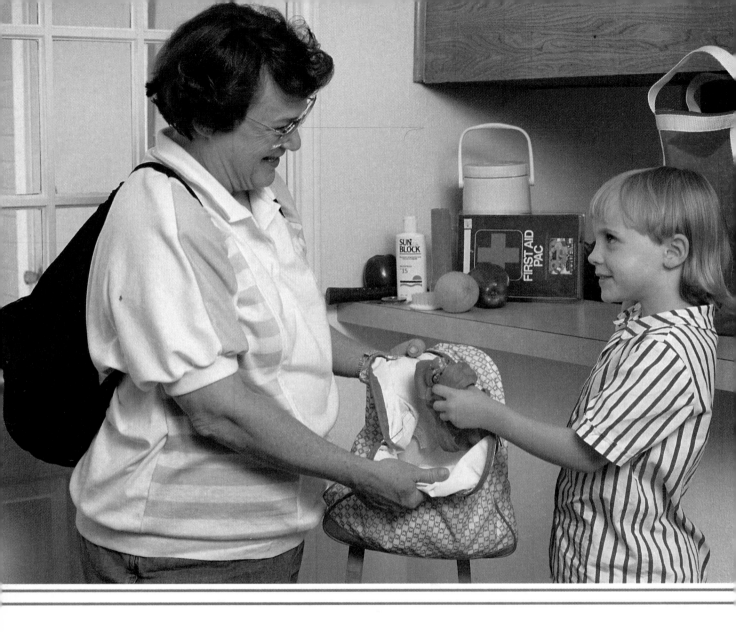

**2**

Sue and Jule will hike to a mine.
Jule fills a huge bag and gets set to hike.
Sue gets her suit and puts it into a bag.

It is a five mile hike to the mine.
It is June and the sun is hot.

3

**4**

Sue and Jule hike in the hot sun.
Can Jule find the mine?

Jule finds the nice lake.
It is a mile from the lake to the mine.

5

**6** Sue puts on her suit and takes a dip.
Jule wades and sits.

Sue and Jule find the mine.
Jule tells Sue the rules to be safe in the mine.

**8**

Sue can not wait to go in the mine!
"I will get lots of gems!" said Sue.
Will Sue and Jule get gems in the mine?

# Just For Fun

Ask someone to help you read and do these activities.

## Finding Long u Words

1. Look through the story to see how many long **u** words you can find.

2. Write the words on a piece of paper. Practice reading the words out loud.

## What Do You Think?

Have someone help you read and answer these questions.

1. What did Sue and Jule like to do?

2. What did Sue put in her bag?

3. How long was the hike to the mine?

4. Do you think Sue and June will find gems in the mine? Why or why not?

STECK
PHONICS READERS
VAUGHN

# Sue and Jule

Phonetically Sequenced Stories in This Set

1. A Race on the Lake
2. The Cake Bake
3. Five Mice and Mike
4. The Big Bike
5. Miss Duke's Mule
6. **Sue and Jule**
7. Mole King Cole and Anna Tole
8. Jo's Toes
9. A Real Seal
10. Hide and Seek

STECK-VAUGHN
C O M P A N Y

ISBN 0-8114-5170-4

90000

9 780811 451703

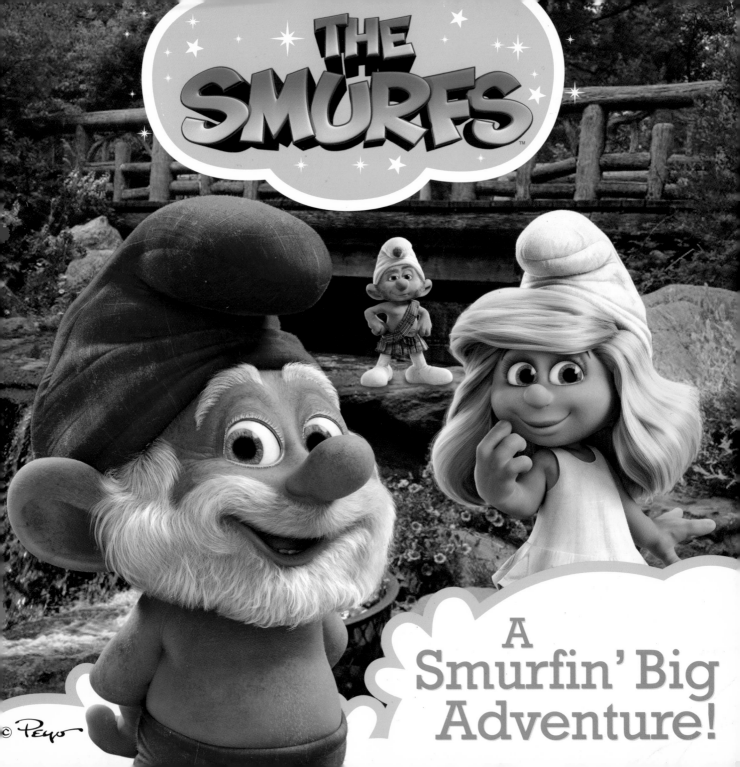